CAMBRIDGE IGCSE CHINESE AS A SECOND LANGUAGE (0523)

2023 MOCK PAPER

PAPER 2 LISTENING

Contents

About the Author: 3

Our Story 5

David's Video Courses in Udemy: 6

David Yao Amazon Kindle Author Central page 7

Books by David YAO at Apple Book Store: 8

Preface - Cambridge IGCSE Chinese 9

   Cambridge IGCSE Chinese - Second Language (0523) 9

      Syllabuses 10

      Paper 1 Reading and Writing 2 hours 10

      Paper 2 Listening Approx. 35–45 minutes 10

      Component 3 Speaking Approx. 10–13 minutes 11

听力 Listening Comprehension 12

   Listening 1 练习一 Question 1-6 12

   Listening 2 练习二 Question 7 19

   Listening 3 练习三 Question 8 (a)–(h) 22

   Listening 3 练习四 Question 9 (a)–(h) 26

Edeo Expanded Explanations 32

   Listening 1 练习一 Question 1-6 32

   Listening 2 练习二 Question 7 41

   Listening 3 练习三 Question 8 (a)–(h) 47

   Listening 3 练习四 Question 9 (a)–(h) 54

More Related Products 更多相关书籍和课程 66

- CIE IGCSE Second Language (0523) 66
  - CIE IGCSE Chinese Second Language (0523) 2020 Specimen Paper 1 Reading and Writing 66
  - CIE IGCSE Chinese Second Language (0523) 2020 Specimen Paper 1 Reading and Writing 67
  - CIE IGCSE Chinese Second Language (0523) 2020 Specimen Paper 2 Listening 67
  - CIE IGCSE Chinese Second Language (0523) 2020 Paper 1 Reading and Writing 68
  - CIE IGCSE Chinese Second Language (0523) 2020 Paper 2 Listening 68
  - CIE IGCSE Chinese (0523) 2019 - Paper 1 Reading and Writing Set 1 69
  - CIE IGCSE Chinese (0523) 2019 - Paper 1 Reading and Writing Set 1 69
  - CIE IGCSE Chinese (0523) 2018 - Paper 1 Reading and Writing Set 1 70
  - CIE IGCSE Chinese (0523) 2017- Paper 1 Reading and Writing Set 1 70
  - CIE IGCSE Chinese (0523) 2016- Paper 1 Reading and Writing Set 1 71
  - CIE IGCSE Chinese (0523) 2015 - Paper 1 Reading and Writing Set 1 71
  - CIE IGCSE Chinese (0523) 2014- Paper 1 Reading and Writing Set 1 72
  - CIE IGCSE Chinese (0523) 2013- Paper 1 Reading and Writing Set 1 72
  - CIE IGCSE Chinese (0523) 2012 - Paper 1 Reading and Writing Set 1 72

We offer more… 73

Design Your Own Program, Customize the Courses using Your Own LOGO 73

We welcome Teachers to join our group! 76

Franchising Program 77
  - Introduction 77
  - Modular Fee Structure 78
  - Training and Supporting 80
  - Marketing and Referral system 82

Tai Chi Fitness Franchising Program 84

About the Author:

David Yao is a highly experienced Mandarin teacher for non-native speakers and the founder of Legoo Mandarin (www.LegooMandarin.com) and Educational Video Courses Online (www.Edeo.biz). Originally from China, he currently resides in Kuala Lumpur, Malaysia and holds a Master's degree from the University of Malaya. With over 26 years of experience in teaching Mandarin to foreigners, David has become an expert in various Mandarin proficiency examinations such as HSK, IB Chinese, IGCSE Chinese, AP Chinese, and SAT Chinese.

David's expertise in Mandarin teaching is reflected in the comprehensive SYSTEM he has developed, consisting of more than 200 Mandarin courses and over 600 books available on Amazon. These materials are specifically designed to cater to the needs of non-native speakers of Chinese. In addition to his Mandarin teaching expertise, David has also expanded his interests to include English and Malaysian languages. He has edited a series of trilingual textbooks and vocabulary books, showcasing his proficiency in all three languages.

David's passion for language teaching has helped thousands of students learn Mandarin, and his innovative teaching methods have made him one of the most sought-after language teachers worldwide. He is known for his dedication to his craft and his ability to help students achieve success in various Mandarin proficiency examinations, whether it's for academic or personal purposes.

David's teaching style is dynamic and tailored to the individual needs of his students. He understands the challenges that non-native speakers face when learning Mandarin and works tirelessly to make the process as smooth as possible. His commitment to his students is evident in the way he takes the time to understand their unique learning styles and create personalized lesson plans to meet their goals.

With a wealth of experience and knowledge, David has established himself as a leader in the field of Mandarin language teaching. His passion and dedication to his students have helped him build a reputation as one of the most respected and effective language teachers worldwide.

He expands his interest and expertise to English and Malaysian Language, editing a series of trilingual textbooks and vocabulary books.

He practices Tai Chi for almost 30 years and establishes Tai Chi Fitness Organization (http://taichifitness.org/) to modernize and promote Tai Chi for fitness and health.

Our Story

"Share with You What We Know Best" is our Slogan. We start with LEGOO Mandarin and now expand the system into other topics: Bahasa Malaysia, IT eCommerce, Accounting and Finance, Tai Chi Fitness and Qi Gong. You can learn anytime anywhere!

In addition to be a **Contents Provider**, we also provide **Online Systems,** which can be easily integrated with your school or company online system or use separately. We are using Udemy and other more than 10 similar platforms for video courses marketing. The Amazon KDP, Google Books and Apple iBooks are platforms we publishing our textbooks in addition to our own platform. We provide consultancy service to save your time and give you the best tips on how to leverage your efforts using all these amazing platforms. Please contact us for quotations (very reasonable price).

We can assign our trained teachers to conduct **live lesson** through Webinar, Skype and YouTube, Facebook at reasonable price.

Licencing Program to schools & Resellers

We offer Licencing Program to schools! More schools are using our system! You can use quiz, video course, PPT and PDF under our Licencing Program. Customized course development with your own LOGO can be done. Please contact us for details and quotations (very reasonable price).

Licencing Program to Resellers

We offer Licencing Program to Resellers, book stores and other

Platforms (Websites, Google stores, Groupons, Facebook stores). We provide contents such PDF books, online Quiz and Video Courses. You can list our contents in your platform. We will share on 50-50 sales basis. We can provide technical assistance to integrate our contents with your system and help response within 24 hours.

Please contact us by whatsapp +60163863716.

David's Video Courses in Udemy:

David Yao Amazon Kindle Author Central page

For Hardcopy or paperback books at best price with reduced postage, please visit: David Yao Amazon Kindle Author Central page:

http://bit.ly/david-amazon-kdp (USA)

Books by David YAO at Apple Book Store:

https://books.apple.com/us/author/david-yao/id584331956

Preface - Cambridge IGCSE Chinese

The International General Certificate of Secondary Education is based examination similar to GCSE and is recognized in the UK as being equivalent to the GCSE for the purposes of recognizing prior attainment. It was developed by University of Cambridge International Examinations. Cambridge programmes and qualifications set the global standard for international education. They are created by subject experts, rooted in academic rigour and reflect the latest educational research.

There are 3 levels for Cambridge IGCSE Chinese:

Cambridge IGCSE Chinese - First Language (0509), similar to A Level (Edexcel GCSE), HSK 6 (Chinese Proficiency Test 6)

Cambridge IGCSE Chinese - Second Language (0523), similar to AS Level (Edexcel GCSE), HSK 5 (Chinese Proficiency Test 5)

Cambridge IGCSE Mandarin Chinese - Foreign Language (0547), similar to Edexcel GCSE (Higer Tier), HSK 4 (Chinese Proficiency Test 4)

Cambridge IGCSE Chinese - Second Language (0523)

Cambridge IGCSE Chinese as a Second Language is designed for learners who already have a working knowledge of the language and who want to consolidate their understanding to progress their education or career. Through their studies, learners achieve a thorough understanding of a wide range of registers and styles and learn to communicate appropriately in different situations.

The syllabus focuses on the linked language skills of reading, writing, listening and oral communication. Through their study of Cambridge IGCSE Chinese as a Second Language, learners can achieve a level of practical communication ideal for everyday use, which can also form the basis for further, more in-depth language study.

Syllabuses

Paper 1 Reading and Writing 2 hours

Written examination consisting of five exercises that test a range of reading and writing skills. Types of task include: information transfer, short-answer questions, multiple-matching, functional writing and extended writing.

Paper 2 Listening Approx. 35–45 minutes

Written examination consisting of four exercises that test listening skills. andidates listen to recordings of short and longer spoken texts. Types of task include: short-answer questions, gap-fill sentences, information correction and multiple-choice questions.

Component 3 Speaking Approx. 10–13 minutes

The Speaking test is conducted in Mandarin Chinese. The Speaking test consists of three parts: candidates give a two- to three-minute presentation, followed by a short discussion with the examiner about the presentation, followed by a short conversation with the examiner about general topics.

By referring to Cambridge IGCSE Chinese, Edexcel IGCSE Chinese (another two examination board) and HSK (Chicness Proficiency Test), combining our 25 years experience in Teaching and editing our own materials. Here is the "LIFE SAVING" book called by many students for their exams. It takes our years' painful effort to edit. The book give a quick revision for your coming exam! Grab it!

听力 Listening Comprehension

R Cambridge Assessment International Education

Cambridge IGCSE June 2023 examination in Chinese as a Second Language.

Paper 2, Listening Comprehension.

Turn over now.

PAUSE 5 SECONDS

Track 1

Listening 1 练习一 Question 1-6

M 练习一，问题一至六

你将听到六段录音，每段录音两遍。请在相应的横线上回答问题一至六。回答应简短扼要。

每段录音后会有停顿。请在停顿期间阅读问题。

PAUSE 45 SECONDS

[SIGNAL]

M 录音一

F * 喂,俊伟。下个星期天是我的生日,你有空来我的生日会吗?

M 当然有空!在森林公园烧烤,是吗?

F 去年聚会的人多,所以在公园,但是,今年就在我家花园喝喝下午茶。

M 好的,我一定准时参加。**

PAUSE 10 SECONDS

Repeat from * to **

PAUSE 5 SECONDS

1 去年女生的生日是在哪儿过的?

.... [1]

M 录音二

F * 各位居民，现在广播安全注意事项：请各家各户在出门前锁好门窗，检查水电煤气的开关是否关好，深夜出行前应该特别注意这些事项。小区服务中心的热线 24 小时开通，如果您有急事或特殊需求，请随时致电服务中心。**

PAUSE 10 SECONDS

Repeat from * to **

PAUSE 5 SECONDS

2 广播特别强调哪个时间段的安全事项？

.... [1]

M 录音三

M * 王老师，我想了解一下关于参加'爱心传递'的义工活动。

F 好的，'爱心传递'是公益组织，鼓励在校学生积极参与社区义工活动，在累计六十个小时以上的义工服务后可以获得银质徽章，累计服务一百个小时以上可以获得金质徽章。

M 好的，我今天就写申请书！**

PAUSE 10 SECONDS

Repeat from * to **

PAUSE 5 SECONDS

3 获得银质徽章需要做多长时间的义工？

.... [1]

M 录音四

F * 您好，我想预定星期六的晚餐，六个人，可以吗？

M 春节期间特别忙，周六七点前没有一个空桌了。

F 请帮我想想办法好吗？周六是我父母的金婚纪念日，意义特殊啊！

M 这个……这个……我尽力但不能保证7点半前有空桌。**

PAUSE 10 SECONDS

Repeat from * to **

PAUSE 5 SECONDS

4 服务员对顾客的要求感到怎么样？

.... [1]

M 录音五

F * 你养过宠物吗?

M 我一直想养狗,可是我家空间很小,一房一厅不太适合养狗。你呢?

F 大家都说宠物会把家里弄得乱糟糟的,不过,我养了两只小狗,一回家它们就跑过来迎接我,一天

的烦恼都没了!

M 我认为动物和人一样都是有情感的**。

PAUSE 10 SECONDS

Repeat from * to **

PAUSE 5 SECONDS

5 男生为什么没有养狗?

.... [1]

M 录音六

F * 俗话说：管住嘴，迈开腿。'管住嘴'说的就是要抵制零食的诱惑。饼干、巧克力的热量很高应该尽量避免。'迈开腿'说得就是适当的运动能加快新陈代谢，提高睡眠质量，增加免疫力。**

PAUSE 10 SECONDS

Repeat from * to **

PAUSE 5 SECONDS

6 人们应该做什么才能睡得更好？

.... [1]

[总分:6]

M: 练习一到此结束

Listening 2 练习二 Question 7

Track 2

M 练习二，问题七

你将听到一段关于《校园手机法》的报道。你将听到两遍。

请听录音，然后回答问题。

请先阅读一下问题。

PAUSE 45 SECONDS

[SIGNAL]

M * 手机的普及改变了人们的学习和工作方式，学生带着手机上学早已不是新鲜事了。社会学家通过研究得出，相比成年人，青少年的自控能力相对较弱。不可否认，手机的确是一个方便快捷的通讯工具，所以'孩子应该不应该带手机进校园'一直是家长和学校老师关注的问题。手机上有各种游戏，视频功能，尤其是社交平台对学习的负面影响显而易见。

记者来到长治实验学校，详细了解这所学校是怎么破解'手机难题'的。这是一所小学，初中，高中一贯制学校。早在2017年就制定了《校园手机法》。根据规定，初中、高中学生们可以带手机进入校园，小学部学生除外。学生必须填写申请书，由家长签名，班主任批准，年级组备案。在校园里学生保证手机处于关机状态，开机时间段是午餐的半小时，初中生 16:30 以后，高中生 17:30 以后。学生在社团活动的时候也可以开机，然而，聊天软件，玩游戏，观看不良视频，在公共场所用扬声器播放手机音乐是严格禁止的。

《校园手机法》是完全'听学生的'，学生们反复讨论、举行听证会然后以投票的方式最终通过并执行。全校学生从一开始就非常配合，目前为止几乎没有学生因为违反规定而受到学校处罚的。学生会主席表示：完全不允许学生带手机进校园的规定不一定是最好的，我们都认为由学生民主参与，互相监督会产生积极的效应！**

PAUSE 30 SECONDS

M 现在请再听一遍

Repeat from * to **

PAUSE 30 SECONDS

M 练习二到此结束

请先阅读一下问题。

(a) 社会学家认为青少年比成年人对手机的 .... 能力差。

(b) 手机上的 .... 对学习有特别不好的影响。

(c) 长治实验学校 .... 部的学生不能带手机进入校园。

(d) 带手机进入学校的申请书必须由 .... 批准。

(e) 初中生下午开手机的时间比高中生 .... 。

(f) 学生们不能在 .... 大声播放手机音乐。

(g)《校园手机法》是学生用 .... 方式来决定的。

(h) 学生会主席认为让学生带手机进校园的规定效果 .... 。

Listening 3 练习三 Question 8 (a)–(h)

M 练习三，问题八

你将听到一段关于联合办公室的播客文章。

你将听到两遍。请根据听到的信息改正每句话里划线的词语。把答案写在括号里。请先阅读一下问题。

PAUSE 45 SECONDS

[SIGNAL]

F * 什么是'联合办公室'？什么样的人在这里工作？三层办公室里藏着50家创业公司，接近300人在这里上班。走进公共区域就能一眼看到墙上六个时区的钟，不过最吸引人的是带着多元文化，说着世界各地语言的人们。据说在这里工作的人来自28个不同的国家。投资人，创业者，留学海归，有年轻的，也有不再年轻的…忙得一刻也停不下来，工作节奏完全和普通办公室不一样！

创业不只是一份工作，它是一种生活方式的选择。法国小伙保罗对记者说："工作就是我热爱的事情，朋友都和我一样，我们享受喝着咖啡，讨论着技术问题直到深夜的时光。"保罗现在在中国做的项目是一个全球性的程序开发，他表示自己一直在往前看，学习最前沿的新技术。

为什么成功人士要离开大公司选择创业呢？投资人蒋先生打了一个比方：大公司就好比是一条大船，员工就是划船人，使劲地划使劲地划，但是不能决定大船要往哪里开。但是自己创业就没什么限制。不过，自己创业更需要合理安排时间。蒋先生把每天的时间分成几个板块，一部分是管理公司的日常运营，一部分必须是留出至少百分之三十的时间用来学习'充电'。他认为公司未来的发展要求一个人拥有全面的技能。

随着出国热出国又随着回国潮回到家乡的小陈对创业有自己的想法："创业刚开始觉得这有什么难的？因为我的家在这里，我会说这里的语言，其实回国创业比我在国外的时候更难，比如家人，同学不一定会理解你支持你。"刚过三十岁的小陈认为年龄就是一个数字而已，不是一个界限，当然很多人希望年轻十岁，因为有更多机会。

在联合办公室里没有朝九晚五的打卡上班，在这里，人们似乎感受不到时间的流逝，空间的间隔。在这里，哪儿都是可以工作的地方。

**

PAUSE 30 SECONDS

M 现在请再听一遍

Repeat from * to **

PAUSE 30 SECONDS

[SIGNAL]

M 练习三到此结束

请先阅读一下问题。

例：在联合办公室里有超过三百人一起工作。

　　在联合办公室里有接近三百人一起工作。

(a) 走进公共区域最吸引人的是不同时区的钟。

　　走进公共区域最吸引人的是不同 (........)。 [1]

(b) 在联合办公室里的工作气氛很轻松。

在联合办公室里的工作气氛很 (........)。 [1]

(c) 法国小伙保罗认为工作是他的负担。

法国小伙保罗认为工作是他的 (........)。 [1]

(d) 保罗现在开发的是一个面向中国市场的程序项目。

保罗现在开发的是一个面向 (........) 的程序项目。 [1]

(e) 人们选择创业是为了有更多的钱。

人们选择创业是为了有更多的(........)。 [1]

(f) 蒋先生认为一个技能不能满足创业初期的要求。

蒋先生认为一个技能不能满足(........) 的要求。 [1]

(g) 小陈刚开始以为回国创业比在国外生活有趣得多。

小陈刚开始以为回国创业比在国外生活(........) 得多。 [1]

(h) 小陈觉得语言不是创业的障碍。

小陈觉得(........)不是创业的障碍。 [1]

[总分:8]

Listening 3 练习四 Question 9 (a)–(h)

Track 4

M 练习四，问题九

你将听到一段对季翔同学的采访记录。

请听下面的采访，你将听到两遍，在唯一正确的方格内打勾（√）回答问题。

请先阅读一下问题。

PAUSE 45 SECONDS

[SIGNAL]

F * 欢迎收看《校园聚焦》节目。今天我们请到了十二年级的季翔同学，请他谈谈他的新发明'智慧小新'。

M 主持人，你好！各位老师好，同学们好。

F 季翔，你手中的这个小玩意儿为什么叫'智慧小新'？

M 这是一个电脑控制的语音系统，它虽然小小的，但是很聪明-可以跟人对话，根据说话人的语音，语调甚至语速来给出相应的答复，很适合'智慧'这个词。我小时候最爱一个动画片叫'铅笔小新'，每次去爷爷家我就会吵着让爷爷给我放'铅笔小新'的CD碟片，所以叫它'智慧小新'再合适不过了。

F 明白了，'小新'是你的童年回忆啊！这个名字真有意思！请你具体说一说吧。

M 我的爷爷今年八十岁了，身体很健康但是很倔强，坚持自己住。妈妈很担心万一爷爷有紧急情况怎么办。于是，爸爸给他买了一部智能手机，连上网络，设置最大字体，一步到位。可还是出状况了！

F 爷爷忘记密码了？还是把手机弄丢了？

M 都不是！他去超市需要出示会员卡，可是到了商店门口怎么按屏幕这个会员卡就是显示不了。爷爷当时急得汗都出来了，他着急，后面排队的人不耐烦，超市员工安抚他别着急。爷爷告诉我们当时就像面临一场大考试，太难啦！

F 高科技真难为老年人啊！

M 不是吗？于是我就想到如果有一个工具不需要书写和触屏就可以输入信息，既能帮助老年人的生

活，还能跟他们聊天解闷。语音不是一个很好的功能吗？

F 你可以给我们演示一下怎么跟'智慧小新'说话吗？

M 好的，对着'智慧小新'重复两遍'小新，小新'远一些也能收到信号，最好是不超过两米的距离，系统自动打开，你可以听到小

新的回答'你好'。然后，你可以问一个问题比如：今天最高温度是多少？

F 太棒了！那么，在紧急情况下，如果老人离'小新'比较远怎么办？

M 这个问题我也考虑到了，市场上已经有戴在手腕上的紧急呼叫器，我正在研究如何把'小新'和手腕呼叫器接起来，这个问题恐怕一个人短时间内很难解决，需要依靠集体的力量。如果有兴趣参与研究的同学，请联系我吧！

F 众人拾柴火焰高，说得就是这个道理。你对'智慧小新'有没有长远的打算？

M 有的，目前，有九成的老人是居家或社区养老，在今后的五年里，中国社会将迈入中度老龄化，居家养老是发展趋势。我想通过我的努力，推广像'智慧小新'这样的科技小助手来方便居家老人，让他们的晚年生活更幸福。

F 季翔，谢谢你的回答！**

PAUSE 30 SECONDS

M 现在请再听一遍

Repeat from * to **

PAUSE 30 SECONDS

M 练习四到此结束，听力考试结束。

R This is the end of the examination

练习四，问题 9(a) - (h)

你将听到一段对季翔同学的采访记录。

请听下面的采访，你将听到两遍，在唯一正确的方格内打勾（□）回答问题。

请先阅读一下问题。

(a) '智慧小新'可以对 做出相应的回答。 [1]

A 语速，口音

B 语调，语速

C 口音，语调

(b) 季翔决定用'小新'这个名字是因为 [1]

A 爷爷和他的回忆。

B 爷爷小时候的朋友。

C 爷爷最爱听的CD。

(c) 爷爷的手机出了什么状况？[1]

A 网络没有了

B 触屏不显示

C 密码丢失了

(d) 超市员工对爷爷是什么态度？[1]

A 尊重

B 无奈

C 同情

(e) 语音功能的特点有哪些？[1]

A 不需要手写和网络

B 不需要触屏和手写

C 不需要充电和触屏

(f) 和'智慧小新'对话的时候应该保持多长距离？[1]

A 两米以内

B 两到三米之间

C 越远越好

(g) 季翔需要什么样的帮助来完善'智慧小新'的功能？[1]

A 研究经费

B 市场调研

C 团队合作

(h) 今后五年里，中国社会老龄化有什么变化？[1]

A 会用高科技的老人越来越多

B 在中等城市的老人越来越多

C 在家养老的老人越来越多

[总分:8]

Edeo Expanded Explanations

R Cambridge Assessment International Education

Cambridge IGCSE June 2023 examination in Chinese as a Second Language.

Paper 2, Listening Comprehension.

Turn over now.

PAUSE 5 SECONDS

Track 1

Listening 1 练习一 Question 1-6

M 练习一，问题一至六

你将听到六段录音，每段录音两遍。请在相应的横线上回答问题一至六。回答应简短扼要。

每段录音后会有停顿。请在停顿期间阅读问题。

You will hear six recordings, each played twice. Please answer questions one to six on the respective lines. Your responses should be brief and concise. There will be a pause after each recording. Please read the questions during the pause.

PAUSE 45 SECONDS

[SIGNAL]

M 录音一

F *喂，俊伟。下个星期天是我的生日，你有空来我的生日会吗？

M 当然有空！在森林公园烧烤，是吗？

F 去年聚会的人多，所以在公园，但是，今年就在我家花园喝喝下午茶。

M 好的，我一定准时参加。**

F: "Hey, Junwei. Next Sunday is my birthday. Do you have time to come to my birthday party?"

M: "Of course, I'm available! We're having a barbecue in the park, right?"

F: "Last year, there were many people, so we had it in the park. But this year, we're just having afternoon tea in my garden."

M: "Alright, I'll definitely be there on time."

PAUSE 10 SECONDS

Repeat from * to **

PAUSE 5 SECONDS

1 去年女生的生日是在哪儿过的？

.....(森林)公园.... [1]

M 录音二

F *各位居民，现在广播安全注意事项：请各家各户在出门前锁好门窗，检查水电煤气的开关是否关好，深夜出行前应该特别注意这些事项。小区服务中心的热线 24 小时开通，如果您有急事或特殊需求，请随时致电服务中心。**

F: "Attention, residents. We are now broadcasting safety precautions: please make sure to lock your doors and windows before leaving your homes. Check that water, electricity, and gas switches are turned off. Pay special attention to these matters if you are going out late at night. The hotline at the community service center is available 24 hours a day.

If you have an emergency or special needs, please feel free to call the service center at any time."

PAUSE 10 SECONDS

Repeat from * to **

PAUSE 5 SECONDS

2 广播特别强调哪个时间段的安全事项？

.... 深夜/晚上/夜晚/夜里/夜间.... [1]

M 录音三

M* 王老师，我想了解一下关于参加'爱心传递'的义工活动。

F 好的，'爱心传递'是公益组织，鼓励在校学生积极参与社区义工活动，在累计[1]六十个小时以上的义工服务后可以获得银质徽章[2]，累计服务一百个小时以上可以获得金质徽章。

M 好的，我今天就写申请书！**

M: "Teacher Wang, I'd like to learn more about participating in the 'Love Relay' volunteer activities."

F: "Sure, 'Love Relay' is a charity organization that encourages students to actively participate in community volunteer work. You can earn a silver badge after accumulating over sixty hours of volunteer service and a gold badge for over one hundred hours of service."

M: "Great, I'll write my application today!"

PAUSE 10 SECONDS

Repeat from * to **

PAUSE 5 SECONDS

3 获得银质徽章需要做多长时间的义工？

.... 六十个小时/60 个小时以上/至少六十小时..... [1]

---

[1] 累计   lěijì   (动) 1 add up (名) 2 accumulative total; grand total   HSK 7-9 V2021

[2] 徽章   huīzhāng   (名) badge; insignia   HSK 12 V2022

M 录音四

F * 您好，我想预定星期六的晚餐，六个人，可以吗？

M 春节期间特别忙，周六七点前没有一个空桌了。

F 请帮我想想办法好吗？周六是我父母的金婚纪念日，意义特殊啊！

M 这个……这个……我尽力但不能保证7点半前有空桌。**

F: "Hello, I'd like to make a reservation for dinner on Saturday for six people, is that possible?"

M: "During the Spring Festival, it's particularly busy, and there are no available tables before 7 o'clock on Saturday."

F: "Can you please try to find a solution? Saturday is my parents' golden wedding anniversary, and it's very special!"

M: "Um... I'll do my best, but I can't guarantee a table before 7:30."

PAUSE 10 SECONDS

Repeat from * to **

PAUSE 5 SECONDS

4 服务员对顾客的要求感到怎么样？

.... 为难 ...... [1]

M 录音五

F * 你养过宠物吗？

M 我一直想养狗，可是我家空间很小，一房一厅不太适合养狗。你呢？

F 大家都说宠物会把家里弄得乱糟糟的，不过，我养了两只小狗，一回家它们就跑过来迎接我，一天的烦恼都没了！

M 我认为动物和人一样都是有情感的**。

F: "Have you ever had pets?"

M: "I've always wanted to have a dog, but my home is small, just one bedroom and one living room, not very suitable for dogs. How about you?"

F: "Everyone says that pets can make the house messy, but I have two small dogs. When I come home, they come running to greet me, and all the day's troubles disappear!"

M: "I believe that animals, like humans, have emotions."

PAUSE 10 SECONDS

Repeat from * to **

PAUSE 5 SECONDS

5 男生为什么没有养狗？

..... 家里(空间)小....... [1]

M 录音六

F * 俗话说：管住嘴，迈开腿。'管住嘴'说的就是要抵制[3]零食的诱惑[4]。饼干、巧克力的热量很高应该尽量避免。'迈开腿'说得就是适当的运动能加快新陈代谢，提高睡眠质量，增加免疫力。**

F: "As the saying goes: 'Control your mouth, get moving.' 'Control your mouth' means resisting the temptation of snacks. Biscuits and chocolates are high in calories and should be avoided as much as possible. 'Get

---

[3] 抵制　　　dǐzhì　(动) resist; boycott HSK 6 V2009 // HSK 7-9 V2021

[4] 诱惑　　　yòuhuò　　(动) 1 entice; tempt; seduce; lure 2 attract; allure; sth is calling you (If something is calling you, you have a strong feeling that you must do it, have it, go there, etc.)   HSK 6 V2009 // HSK 7-9 V2021

moving' means that appropriate exercise can speed up metabolism, improve the quality of sleep, and boost your immune system."

PAUSE 10 SECONDS

Repeat from * to **

PAUSE 5 SECONDS

6 人们应该做什么才能睡得更好？

....(适当)运动/迈开腿/锻炼.... [1]

[总分:6]

M: 练习一到此结束

Listening 2 练习二 Question 7

Track 2

M 练习二，问题七

你将听到一段关于《校园手机法》的报道。你将听到两遍。

请听录音，然后回答问题。

请先阅读一下问题。

You will hear a report about the "Campus Mobile Phone Act." You will hear it twice. Please listen to the recording and then answer the questions. Please read the questions first.

PAUSE 45 SECONDS

[SIGNAL]

M * 手机的普及改变了人们的学习和工作方式，学生带着手机上学早已不是新鲜事了。社会学家通过研究得出，相比成年人，青少年的自控能力相对较弱。不可否认，手机的确是一个方便快捷的通讯工具，所以'孩子应该不应该带手机进校园'一直是家长和学校老师关注的问题。手机上有各种游戏，视频功能，尤其是社交平台对学习的负面影响显而易见[5]。

M: "The proliferation of mobile phones has changed the way people study and work, and students bringing phones to school is no longer a novelty. Sociologists have found through research that compared to adults, teenagers have relatively weaker self-control. It's undeniable that mobile phones are indeed convenient and efficient communication tools.

---

[5] 显而易见 xiǎn'éryìjiàn (副) obviously; evidently: 明显而容易见到 HSK 7-9 V2021

Therefore, whether 'children should or should not bring phones to campus' has always been a concern for parents and school teachers. Phones have various games, video functions, and, especially, the negative impact of social media on learning is obvious.

记者来到长治实验学校，详细了解这所学校是怎么破解'手机难题'的。这是一所小学，初中，高中一贯制学校。早在2017年就制定了《校园手机法》。根据规定，初中、高中学生们可以带手机进入校园，小学部学生除外。学生必须填写申请书，由家长签名，班主任批准，年级组备案。在校园里学生保证手机处于关机状态，开机时间段是午餐的半小时，初中生16:30以后，高中生17:30以后。学生在社团活动的时候也可以开机，然而，聊天软件，玩游戏，观看不良视频，在公共场所用扬声器播放手机音乐是严格禁止的。

A reporter visited Changzhi Experimental School to understand how this school is addressing the 'mobile phone challenge.' This is a school that includes primary, junior high, and senior high levels. As early as 2017, they formulated the 'Campus Mobile Phone Act.' According to the regulations, junior high and senior high school students can bring their phones into the campus, with the exception of primary school students. Students must fill out an application, signed by parents, approved by the class teacher, and recorded by the grade team. Students must ensure that their phones are turned off on campus. The allowed times for turning them on are half an hour during lunch, 4:30 PM for junior high students, and 5:30 PM for senior high students. Students can also turn on their phones during extracurricular activities. However, using chat apps, playing games, watching inappropriate videos, and playing phone music with speakers in public places are strictly prohibited.

《校园手机法》是完全'听学生的',学生们反复讨论、举行听证会然后以投票的方式最终通过并执行。全校学生从一开始就非常配合,目前为止几乎没有学生因为违反规定而受到学校处罚的。学生会主席表示:完全不允许学生带手机进校园的规定不一定是最好的,我们都认为由学生民主参与,互相监督会产生积极的效应!**

The 'Campus Mobile Phone Act' is entirely 'student-driven.' Students discussed it repeatedly, held hearings, and finally passed it through a vote and implemented it. The whole school's students have been very cooperative from the beginning. So far, almost no students have been punished by the school for violating the rules. The student council president stated: 'The rule that absolutely does not allow students to bring phones to campus is not necessarily the best. We all believe that rules formed through students' democratic participation and mutual supervision will have a positive effect!'"

PAUSE 30 SECONDS

M 现在请再听一遍

Repeat from * to **

PAUSE 30 SECONDS

M 练习二到此结束

请先阅读一下问题。

(a) 社会学家认为青少年比成年人对手机的(自控/自控能力能力)差。

(a) Sociologists believe that teenagers have poorer self-control over phones compared to adults.

(b) 手机上的(社交平台)对学习有特别不好的影响。

(b) Social media platforms on phones have a particularly negative impact on learning.

(c) 长治实验学校(小学/小学生)部的学生不能带手机进入校园。

(c) Students of the primary school section at Changzhi Experimental School cannot bring phones onto the campus.

(d) 带手机进入学校的申请书必须由(班主任/班导师)批准。

(d) The application to bring phones into the school must be approved by the class teacher.

(e) 初中生下午开手机的时间比高中生(早/长/多/早一个小时/早一个钟/多一个小时/(提)前一个小时)。

(e) Junior high students are allowed to turn on their phones in the afternoon an hour earlier than high school students.

(f) 学生们不能在(公共场所/公共区域/公共场合)大声播放手机音乐。

(f) Students are not allowed to play phone music loudly in public places.

(g) 《校园手机法》是学生用(投票(的))方式来决定的。

(g) The "Campus Mobile Phone Act" was decided by students through a voting process.

(h) 学生会主席认为让学生带手机进校园的规定效果(很不错/很好/积极/好/显著)。

(h) The Student Council President believes that the regulation allowing students to bring phones to the campus has a positive effect.

Listening 3 练习三 Question 8 (a)–(h)

M 练习三，问题八

你将听到一段关于联合办公室的播客文章。

你将听到两遍。请根据听到的信息改正每句话里划线的词语。把答案写在括号里。请先阅读一下问题。

You will hear a podcast article about co-working spaces. You will hear it twice. Please correct the underlined words in each sentence based on the information you hear. Write your answers in parentheses. Please read the questions first.

PAUSE 45 SECONDS

[SIGNAL]

F * 什么是'联合办公室'？什么样的人在这里工作？三层办公室里藏着50家创业公司，接近300人在这里上班。走进公共区域就能一眼看到墙上六个时区的钟，不过最吸引人的是带着多元文化，说着世界各地语言的人们。据说在这里工作的人来自28个不同的国家。投资人，创业者，留学海归[6]，有年轻的，也有不再年轻的…忙得一刻也停不下来，工作节奏完全和普通办公室不一样！

F: What is a 'co-working space'? What kind of people work here? There are 50 startup companies hidden in a three-story office building, with nearly 300 people working here. As you enter the common area, you can instantly see six clocks on the wall displaying different time zones, but the most attractive aspect is the people from diverse cultures who speak various languages from around the world. It is said that people working here come from 28 different countries. Investors, entrepreneurs, overseas returnees, young and not-so-young individuals, all are busy and the work pace is entirely different from a regular office!

---

[6] 海待　　Hǎidài　　(名) overseas educated, overseas returnee who is waiting for a job offer or jobless. 简单解释，就是海外留学归来，却找不到工作的待业者。（谐音"海带" Homophone for "tseaweed；kelp"）

创业不只是一份工作，它是一种生活方式的选择。法国小伙保罗对记者说："工作就是我热爱的事情，朋友都和我一样，我们享受喝着咖啡，讨论着技术问题直到深夜的时光。"保罗现在在中国做的项目是一个全球性的程序开发，他表示自己一直在往前看，学习最前沿的新技术。Entrepreneurship is not just a job; it's a lifestyle choice. A Frenchman named Paul told the reporter, "Work is what I love. Friends are just like me; we enjoy drinking coffee and discussing technical issues until late at night." Paul is currently working on a global programming project in China and says he is always looking ahead, learning the latest cutting-edge technology.

为什么成功人士要离开大公司选择创业呢？投资人蒋先生打了一个比方：大公司就好比是一条大船，员工就是划船人，使劲地划使劲地划，但是不能决定大船要往哪里开。但是自己创业就没什么限制。不过，自己创业更需要合理安排时间。蒋先生把每天的时间分成几个板块，一部分是管理公司的日常运营，一部分必须是留出至少百分之三十的时间用来学习'充电'。他认为公司未来的发展要求一个人拥有全面的技能。Why do successful people leave large companies to start their own businesses? An investor, Mr. Jiang, gave an analogy: a large company is like a big ship, and employees are the rowers. They row with all their might, but they can't decide where the big ship is headed. But when you start your own business, there are no such limitations. However, starting your own business requires better time management. Mr. Jiang divides his day into several blocks; part of it is for managing the company's daily operations, and at least 30% of his time is set aside for 'recharging' or learning. He believes that the future development of the company requires a person to have a wide range of skills.

随着出国热出国又随着回国潮回到家乡的小陈对创业有自己的想法："创业刚开始觉得这有什么难的？因为我的家在这里，我会说这里的语言，其实回国创业比我在国外的时候更难，比如家人，同学不一定会理解你支持你。"刚过三十岁的小陈认为年龄就是一个数字而已，不是一个界限，当然很多人希望年轻十岁，因为有更多机会。As the trend of going abroad has followed by a trend of returning to their hometowns, a young person named Xiao Chen has his own thoughts on entrepreneurship: "At the beginning of starting a business, I thought, 'What's so difficult about it?' Because my home is here, I can speak the local language. In fact, starting a business in my home country is more challenging than when I was abroad. For example, family members and classmates may not necessarily understand and support you." Xiao Chen, who is just over 30, believes that age is just a number, not a limit, although many people wish they were ten years younger because of more opportunities.

在联合办公室里没有朝九晚五[7]的打卡上班，在这里，人们似乎感受不到时间的流逝，空间的间隔。在这里，哪儿都是可以工作的地方。** In a co-working space, there are no strict 9-to-5 working hours. Here, people seem not to feel the passing of time and the constraints of physical space. In this environment, any place can be a workspace.

PAUSE 30 SECONDS

M 现在请再听一遍

Repeat from * to **

PAUSE 30 SECONDS

[SIGNAL]

M 练习三到此结束

例：在联合办公室里有超过三百人一起工作。

---

[7] 朝九晚五 Cháo jiǔ wǎn wǔ   nine-to-five; 9 to 5; nine to five; office space

50 | Page

在联合办公室里有接近三百人一起工作。

(a) 走进公共区域最吸引人的是不同时区的钟。[1]

走进公共区域最吸引人的是不同 (国家/地区的人(们))。

(b) 在联合办公室里的工作气氛很轻松。[1]

在联合办公室里的工作气氛很 (忙(碌[8])/繁忙)。

(c) 法国小伙保罗认为工作是他的负担。[1]

法国小伙保罗认为工作是他的 (乐趣/快乐/享受/热爱(的事情))。

(d) 保罗现在开发的是一个面向中国市场的程序项目。[1]

保罗现在开发的是一个面向 (全球市场/全球性/全世界/国际) 的程序项目。

---

[8] 忙碌　　mánglù　　(形) busy; bustling about HSK 6 V2009 // HSK 7-9 V2021

(e) 人们选择创业是为了有更多的钱。[1]

人们选择创业是为了有更多的(自由/自由度)。

(f) 蒋先生认为一个技能不能满足创业初期的要求。[1]

蒋先生认为一个技能不能满足((公司)未来发展)的要求。

(g) 小陈刚开始以为回国创业比在国外生活有趣得多。[1]

小陈刚开始以为回国创业比在国外生活(简单/容易)得多。

(h) 小陈觉得语言不是创业的障碍。[1]

小陈觉得(年龄/年纪/岁数)不是创业的障碍。

[总分:8]

Listening 3 练习四 Question 9 (a)–(h)

Track 4

M 练习四，问题九

你将听到一段对季翔同学的采访记录。

请听下面的采访，你将听到两遍，在唯一正确的方格内打勾（√）回答问题。

请先阅读一下问题。

PAUSE 45 SECONDS

[SIGNAL]

F * 欢迎收看《校园聚焦》节目。今天我们请到了十二年级的季翔同学，请他谈谈他的新发明'智慧小新'。

F: Welcome to "Campus Focus." Today, we have invited Ji Xiang, a senior student, to talk about his new invention, "Smart Xiao Xin."

M 主持人，你好！各位老师好，同学们好。

M: Hello, everyone, and hello to the teachers and fellow students.

F 季翔，你手中的这个小玩意儿为什么叫'智慧小新'？

F: Ji Xiang, why is this little device in your hand called "Smart Xiao Xin"?

M 这是一个电脑控制的语音系统，它虽然小小的，但是很聪明-可以跟人对话，根据说话人的语音，语调甚至语速来给出相应的答复，很适合'智慧'这个词。我小时候最爱一个动画片叫'铅笔小新'，每次去爷爷家我就会吵着让爷爷给我放'铅笔小新'的CD碟片，所以叫它'智慧小新'再合适不过了。

M: This is a computer-controlled voice system. It may be small, but it's quite smart. It can have conversations with people and provide responses based on the speaker's voice, tone, and even speaking speed. It's suitable for the word "smart." When I was a kid, I loved an animated series called "Crayon Shin-chan." Every time I went to my grandpa's house, I would ask him to play the "Crayon Shin-chan" CD for me. So, I named it "Smart Xiao Xin," which fits perfectly.

F 明白了，'小新'是你的童年回忆啊！这个名字真有意思！请你具体说一说吧。

F: I see, "Xiao Xin" holds a special place in your childhood memories! That's an interesting name. Can you tell us more about it?

M 我的爷爷今年八十岁了，身体很健康但是很倔强[9]，坚持自己住。妈妈很担心万一爷爷有紧急情况怎么办。于是，爸爸给他买了一部智能手机，连上网络，设置最大字体，一步到位。可还是出状况[10]了！

M: My grandpa is eighty years old now, and he's in good health but quite stubborn. He insists on living by himself. My mom was worried about what would happen in case of an emergency. So, my dad got him a smartphone, connected to the internet, with the largest font size, a one-step solution. But he still faced issues!

F 爷爷忘记密码了？还是把手机弄丢了？

F: Did your grandpa forget his password? Or did he lose the phone?

[9] 倔强　　juéjiàng　　(动) (倔犟) stubborn; stubborn, unbending　　HSK 7-9 V2021

[10] 出状况　chū zhuàngkuàng　"出状况" (chū zhuàngkuàng) is a Chinese phrase that can be translated to "encounter problems" or "experience issues." It is used to describe a situation where something doesn't go as planned or expected, and difficulties or unexpected events occur. It can refer to various types of problems or disruptions in different contexts.

M 都不是！他去超市需要出示会员卡，可是到了商店门口怎么按屏幕这个会员卡就是显示不了。爷爷当时急得汗都出来了，他着急，后面排队的人不耐烦，超市员工安抚他别着急。爷爷告诉我们当时就像面临一场大考试，太难啦！

M: It was neither! He needed to show his membership card at the supermarket, but when he got to the store's entrance, he couldn't display the virtual card on the screen. My grandpa was so anxious, and he started sweating. He was in a hurry, the people behind him were getting impatient, and the supermarket staff had to calm him down. He told us it felt like facing a major exam, and it was too difficult!

F 高科技真难为老年人啊！

F: High-tech can be quite challenging for older people!

M 不是吗？于是我就想到如果有一个工具不需要书写和触屏就可以输入信息，既能帮助老年人的生活，还能跟他们聊天解闷[11]。语音不是一个很好的功能吗？

---

[11] 解闷　　jiěmèn　　(动) divert oneself from boredom　　HSK 12 V2022

M: Indeed! So, I thought about creating a tool that doesn't require writing or touchscreen input, one that could assist older people in their daily lives and keep them company. Voice interaction seemed like a great feature.

F 你可以给我们演示一下怎么跟'智慧小新'说话吗?

F: Can you demonstrate how to talk to "Smart Xiao Xin"?

M 好的,对着'智慧小新'重复两遍'小新,小新'远一些也能收到信号,最好是不超过两米的距离,系统自动打开,你可以听到小新的回答'你好'。然后,你可以问一个问题比如:今天最高温度是多少?

M: Of course, just say "Xiao Xin, Xiao Xin" twice, and from a reasonable distance, it can pick up the signal. Ideally, the distance shouldn't exceed two meters. The system will automatically activate, and you'll hear Xiao Xin's response, "Hello." Then, you can ask a question, like, "What's the highest temperature today?"

F 太棒了!那么,在紧急情况下,如果老人离'小新'比较远怎么办?

F: That's amazing! But what if an elderly person is far from "Xiao Xin" during an emergency?

M 这个问题我也考虑到了，市场上已经有戴在手腕上的紧急呼叫器，我正在研究如何把'小新'和手腕呼叫器接起来，这个问题恐怕一个人短时间内很难解决，需要依靠集体的力量。如果有兴趣参与研究的同学，请联系我吧！

M: I've thought about this issue as well. There are already emergency call wristbands available on the market. I'm researching how to integrate "Smart Xiao Xin" with these wristbands. This is a complex problem that might require collective effort to solve. If any students are interested in participating in the research, please reach out to me!

F 众人拾柴火焰高，说得就是这个道理。你对'智慧小新'有没有长远的打算？

F: Many hands make light work. Do you have long-term plans for "Smart Xiao Xin"?

M 有的，目前，有九成的老人是居家或社区养老，在今后的五年里，中国社会将迈入中度老龄化，居家养老是发展趋势。我想通过我的努力，推广像'智慧小新'这样的科技小助手来方便居家老人，让他们的晚年生活更幸福。

M: I do. Currently, 90% of elderly people receive care at home or in the community. In the next five years, China will enter a period of moderate aging, and home-based care is the development trend. I want to promote the use of technology assistants like "Smart Xiao Xin" to make life easier for elderly people in their later years, making their lives happier.

F 季翔，谢谢你的回答！**

F: Ji Xiang, thank you for your answers!

PAUSE 30 SECONDS

M 现在请再听一遍

Repeat from * to **

PAUSE 30 SECONDS

M 练习四到此结束，听力考试结束。

R This is the end of the examination

练习四，问题 9(a) - (h)

你将听到一段对季翔同学的采访记录。

请听下面的采访，你将听到两遍，在唯一正确的方格内打勾（√）回答问题。

请先阅读一下问题。

(a) '智慧小新' 可以对 做出相应的回答。[1]

A 语速，口音

B 语调，语速 √

C 口音，语调

(a) "Smart Xiao Xin" can provide corresponding responses based on what?

A Speed and accent

B Tone, speed √

C Accent and tone

(b) 季翔决定用'小新'这个名字是因为 [1]

A 爷爷和他的回忆。√

B 爷爷小时候的朋友。

C 爷爷最爱听的CD。

(b) Ji Xiang decided to use the name "Xiao Xin" because of what?

A His grandpa and his memories.

B His grandpa's childhood friends.

C His grandpa's favorite CD. ✓

(c) 爷爷的手机出了什么状况？[1]

A 网络没有了

B 触屏不显示 ✓

C 密码丢失了

(c) What issue did Ji Xiang's grandpa face with his smartphone?

A Lost network

B Touchscreen not displaying ✓

C Forgotten password

(d) 超市员工对爷爷是什么态度？ [1]

A 尊重

B 无奈

C 同情 √

(d) How did the supermarket staff react to Ji Xiang's grandpa?

A Respect

B Helplessness

C Sympathy √

(e) 语音功能的特点有哪些？ [1]

A 不需要手写和网络

B 不需要触屏和手写 √

C 不需要充电和触屏

(e) What are the characteristics of the voice function?

A No need for handwriting and the internet

B No need for touchscreen and handwriting √

C No need for charging and touchscreen

(f) 和'智慧小新'对话的时候应该保持多长距离？ [1]

A 两米以内 √

B 两到三米之间

C 越远越好

(f) What distance should be maintained while conversing with "Smart Xiao Xin"?

A Within two meters √

B Between two and three meters

C The farther, the better

(g) 季翔需要什么样的帮助来完善'智慧小新'的功能？ [1]

A 研究经费

B 市场调研

C 团队合作 √

(g) What kind of help does Ji Xiang need to improve "Smart Xiao Xin's" features?

A Research funding

B Market research

C Team cooperation ✓

(h) 今后五年里，中国社会老龄化有什么变化？[1]

A 会用高科技的老人越来越多

B 在中等城市的老人越来越多

C 在家养老的老人越来越多 ✓

(h) What changes are expected in China's aging population in the next five years?

A An increase in tech-savvy elderly people

B A rise in the elderly population in medium-sized cities

C A growth in elderly people opting for home-based care ✓

[总分:8]

More Related Products 更多相关书籍和课程

Our all-in-one Shopify shop offers a wide range of books at the best prices, so you can read more for less @ https://1salesforce.com/

CIE IGCSE Second Language (0523)

CIE IGCSE Chinese Second Language (0523) 2020 Specimen Paper 1 Reading and Writing

- PDF eBook
- Best Price and Details @ http://edeo.biz/26623
- For Hardcopy or Paperback books at best price with reduced postage, please visit: Our Amazon Kindle Author Central page:

http://bit.ly/david-amazon-kdp, using ISBN or ASIN to search the book, Kindle eBook LIVE USD $9.90; ASIN: B08H1VD5BG; Paperback Submitted on September 5, 2020 $12.99 USD ASIN: B08HGZK6WQ ISBN: 9798681155966

CIE IGCSE Chinese Second Language (0523) 2020 Specimen Paper 1 Reading and Writing

- Online Video Course with details explanations
- Best Price and Details @ coming soon

CIE IGCSE Chinese Second Language (0523) 2020 Specimen Paper 2 Listening

- PDF eBook
- Best Price and Details @ http://edeo.biz/26636
- For Hardcopy or Paperback books at best price with reduced postage, please visit: Our Amazon Kindle Author Central page: http://bit.ly/david-amazon-kdp, using ISBN or ASIN to search the book, Kindle eBook $9.90 USD ASIN: B08H2JKHBQ ; Paperback Submitted on September 3, 2020 $12.99 USD ASIN: B08HBKQ35Y ISBN: 9798681335191

CIE IGCSE Chinese Second Language (0523) 2020 Paper 1 Reading and Writing

- PDF eBook

- Best Price and Details @ http://edeo.biz/27821

- For Hardcopy or Paperback books at best price with reduced postage, please visit: Our Amazon Kindle Author Central page: http://bit.ly/david-amazon-kdp, using ISBN or ASIN to search the book, Kindle eBook Submitted on December 26, 2020 $12.99 USD ASIN: B08RC8NJLT ; Paperback Submitted on December 28, 2020 $12.99 USD ASIN: B08RC6LD3G ISBN: 9798586949325

CIE IGCSE Chinese Second Language (0523) 2020 Paper 2 Listening

- PDF eBook

- Best Price and Details @ http://edeo.biz/27848

- For Hardcopy or Paperback books at best price with reduced postage, please visit: Our Amazon Kindle Author Central page: http://bit.ly/david-amazon-kdp, using ISBN or ASIN to search the book, Kindle eBook $12.99 USD ASIN: B08RF1SDQ9 ;

Paperback Submitted on December 30, 2020 $12.99 USD ASIN: B08RR68N5J   ISBN: 9798587588073

CIE IGCSE Chinese (0523) 2019 - Paper 1 Reading and Writing Set 1

- Online Video Course with details explanations
- Best Price and Details @ https://www.udemy.com/course/video-cambridge-igcse-chinese-as-second-language-0523-2019/?referralCode=DF70ED67419F89FDF1B3

CIE IGCSE Chinese (0523) 2019 - Paper 1 Reading and Writing Set 1

- PDF eBook
- Best Price and Details @ http://edeo.biz/26650
- For Hardcopy or Paperback books at best price with reduced postage, please visit: Our Amazon Kindle Author Central page: http://bit.ly/david-amazon-kdp, using ISBN or ASIN to search the book, Paperback Submitted on August 13, 2020 $12.99 USD ASIN: B08FP2BNS6 ;   ISBN: 9798673502952

CIE IGCSE Chinese (0523) 2018 - Paper 1 Reading and Writing Set 1

- PDF eBook

- Best Price and Details @ http://edeo.biz/27981

- For Hardcopy or Paperback books at best price with reduced postage, please visit: Our Amazon Kindle Author Central page: http://bit.ly/david-amazon-kdp, using ISBN or ASIN to search the book, Kindle eBook $12.99 USD ASIN: B08SJ91TLY ; Paperback Submitted on January 9, 2021, $12.99 USD ASIN: B08SGXMP2S ISBN: 9798592105319

CIE IGCSE Chinese (0523) 2017- Paper 1 Reading and Writing Set 1

- PDF eBook

- Best Price and Details @ http://edeo.biz/28062

- For Hardcopy or Paperback books at best price with reduced postage, please visit: Our Amazon Kindle Author Central page: http://bit.ly/david-amazon-kdp, using ISBN or ASIN to search the book, Kindle eBook Submitted on January 13, 2021 $12.99 USD ASIN: B08SW61M98; Paperback Submitted on January 14, 2021; $12.99 USD ASIN: B08SZ6GR9Y , ISBN: 9798594356511

CIE IGCSE Chinese (0523) 2016- Paper 1 Reading and Writing Set 1

- PDF eBook

- Best Price and Details @ http://edeo.biz/28180

- For Hardcopy or Paperback books at best price with reduced postage, please visit: Our Amazon Kindle Author Central page: http://bit.ly/david-amazon-kdp, using ISBN or ASIN to search the book, Kindle eBook $12.99 USD ASIN: B08VJJJK1Y ; Paperback Submitted on February 2, 2021 $12.99 USD ASIN: B08VM1KMMD ISBN: 9798703176993

CIE IGCSE Chinese (0523) 2015 - Paper 1 Reading and Writing Set 1

- PDF eBook

- Best Price and Details @ http://edeo.biz/28338

- For Hardcopy or Paperback books at best price with reduced postage, please visit: Our Amazon Kindle Author Central page: http://bit.ly/david-amazon-kdp, using ISBN or ASIN to search the book, Kindle eBook $12.99 USD ASIN: B08W42V3YT ; Paperback Submitted on February 7, 2021, $12.99 USD ASIN: B08W4ZHPTZ ISBN: 9798705836857

CIE IGCSE Chinese (0523) 2014- Paper 1 Reading and Writing Set 1

- ➢ PDF eBook

- ➢ Best Price and Details @ Coming soon

- ➢ For Hardcopy or Paperback books at best price with reduced postage, please visit: Our Amazon Kindle Author Central page: http://bit.ly/david-amazon-kdp, using ISBN or ASIN to search the book,

CIE IGCSE Chinese (0523) 2013- Paper 1 Reading and Writing Set 1

- ➢ PDF eBook

- ➢ Best Price and Details @ Coming soon

- ➢ For Hardcopy or Paperback books at best price with reduced postage, please visit: Our Amazon Kindle Author Central page: http://bit.ly/david-amazon-kdp, using ISBN or ASIN to search the book,

CIE IGCSE Chinese (0523) 2012 - Paper 1 Reading and Writing Set 1

- ➢ PDF eBook

- ➢ Best Price and Details @ Coming soon

> For Hardcopy or Paperback books at best price with reduced postage, please visit: Our Amazon Kindle Author Central page: http://bit.ly/david-amazon-kdp, using ISBN or ASIN to search the book,

We offer more...

Design Your Own Program, Customize the Courses using Your Own LOGO

- Professional book design using Microsoft Words, with Content, footnotes to explain vocab, grammar etc.

- Convert your school teaching material into the Professional one!

- Convert your school teaching material into PDF file with your own LOGO as watermark

- Protect your PDF files using our know-how skill to prevent copy!

- Save your time on teaching!

- Engage and encourage your students

- Using Microsoft Words file for classroom presentation or Online teaching in a creative way you may never heard

-Convert Microsoft Words document into Video (with background music or narrations)

-Create PPT file for classroom presentation or Online teaching

-Customize the courses using your own LOGO.,

-Create the Promotion Video like a Pro!

-Publish and sell your books (eBook or Paperback book) in Amazon, Google Play Books, and Apple Books as Pro. Your Name will be Author or Co Author

-Publish and sell your Video course on Udemy

-Create online Quiz and auto-grading, save your time in teaching and assessing

-Share Quiz with your students and engaging

-Share your works through social media platform

-Give and control access for your own students

-Easy to integrate the online system with your school system or your social media platform

-Keep using and updating!

-Worry free, hand free, just enjoy your life... AI and automation will help your teaching!

-Build up your own ecommerce Website

-Franchising opportunity

-Online Teaching Tips and Skills

-Social Media Marketing

-online quiz

-Systematic organize your materials for online teaching and sharing.

We welcome Teachers to join our group!

We welcome teacher to join our Facebook group: Chinese Course book, Video Course Design, Research and sharing 中文海外教材教程研究.

Edeo (Educational Video Online Courses) is one of the pioneering online Courses Creators. We provide Contents and Solutions, online, offline, in Classroom presentation or online lessons, group assignments or personal learning management. We welcome Teachers to join our group and marketing networks (more than 1 million users in our networks and social media, YouTube, Udemy, Amazon, iBook, Teachlr, Google Books, Rakuten Kobo etc.) for:

- Developing and publishing books, teaching materials

- Creating and marketing online Video

- Hosting online live courses

https://www.facebook.com/groups/2896012267340830/

Franchising Program

Welcome to the Edeo (Educational Video Online Courses) Franchising Program!

Introduction

At Edeo, we are a renowned provider of online courses, specializing in Mandarin language learning. Our flagship program, LEGOO Mandarin, offers a comprehensive range of materials, including PPT, PDF, and video resources, meticulously designed to cater to learners of all proficiency levels. From Kindergarten and Youth Chinese Test (YCT) to Chinese Proficiency Test (HSK), IGCSE Chinese, A1, A2 Chinese, IB Chinese, SAT Chinese, AP Chinese, and more, our materials cover a wide spectrum of Chinese language education.

With over 27 years of experience in teaching Chinese to foreigners, we have refined our teaching methods to perfection. LEGOO Mandarin is the result of our unwavering dedication to providing top-quality educational content that is both engaging and effective. Our slogan, "Share with You What We Know Best," encapsulates our commitment to sharing our expertise with learners worldwide.

We also offer trained teachers who can conduct live lessons through webinars, Skype, YouTube, and Facebook at a reasonable cost, providing interactive and engaging learning experiences for students.

For schools, we have a licensing program that grants access to our quiz, video courses, PPT, and PDF materials. This program allows you to utilize our resources under our licensing terms, and we can even develop customized courses with your school's branding. Please reach out to us for further details and quotations at a highly competitive price. Additionally, our technical support team is available to assist you in integrating our content with your system, ensuring a seamless user experience. We guarantee a response within 24 hours. Contact us via WhatsApp at +60163863716 to learn more about this opportunity.

Join the Edeo Franchising Program and become a part of our successful journey in providing quality online education. Together, we can empower learners worldwide and make a positive impact on their language learning journey.

Modular Fee Structure

Our Franchising Program fee is charged on a module basis, ensuring that you only pay for the specific modules you choose. This approach offers several advantages, including lower franchising fees and greater flexibility as your business grows. By selecting the modules that align with your target market and goals, you can optimize your investment and maximize your potential for success.

We understand that every franchisee has unique requirements and business objectives. With our modular fee structure, you have the freedom to customize your franchise package based on your specific needs. Whether you want to focus on a particular proficiency level, age group, or specialized curriculum, our flexible pricing model allows you to tailor your investment accordingly.

As you expand and diversify your offerings over time, you can easily add new modules to your franchise package. This ensures that your franchise remains dynamic and adaptable, enabling you to meet the evolving demands of your market and stay ahead of the competition.

Our commitment to transparency and fairness is reflected in our module-based fee system. You can have peace of mind knowing that your franchising fees are directly tied to the modules you choose, providing a clear understanding of your investment and its corresponding returns. We believe in fostering a mutually beneficial partnership where your success is our success.

By offering a flexible and cost-effective franchising fee structure, we aim to empower franchisees like you to thrive in the competitive educational market. We are dedicated to supporting your growth and providing you with the necessary tools and resources to build a successful Mandarin learning franchise.

Join our Franchising Program today and take advantage of our module-based fee system, allowing you to lower your initial investment, increase your flexibility, and unlock the full potential of your franchise. Let us embark on this exciting journey together and make a positive impact on the world of Mandarin language education.

Training and Supporting

Our Franchising Program goes beyond providing you with exceptional educational content and a flexible fee structure. We also offer comprehensive training programs and annual seminar gatherings to support your success as a franchisee.

Through our online training system, you will have access to a wealth of resources that will equip you with the knowledge and skills needed to effectively manage and promote your Mandarin learning program. The training modules cover various aspects, including curriculum implementation, marketing strategies, operational guidelines, customer service excellence, and more. These modules are designed to empower you with the expertise and confidence to deliver a high-quality educational experience to your students.

In addition to the online training, we also organize annual seminar gatherings where franchisees from around the world come together to share their experiences, best practices, and insights. This collaborative environment provides a valuable platform for networking, learning from each other, and gaining fresh perspectives on program management and marketing. You will have the opportunity to connect with fellow franchisees, exchange ideas, and build relationships that can further enhance your success.

We believe in the power of knowledge sharing and the collective wisdom of our franchise community. By fostering an environment of collaboration and continuous learning, we aim to create a supportive ecosystem where franchisees can thrive and grow together. Our commitment to your success goes beyond just providing educational materials; we are dedicated to nurturing your expertise and helping you excel in all aspects of running your Mandarin learning program.

Join our Franchising Program and gain access to our comprehensive training programs and annual seminar gatherings. Through these initiatives, you will not only enhance your skills and knowledge but also have the opportunity to connect with like-minded professionals in the field. Together, we can achieve remarkable results and make a lasting impact on Mandarin language education.

Take the next step in your franchising journey and seize the opportunity to learn, share, and succeed with Edeo's Franchising Program.

Marketing and Referral system

As a franchisor, we understand the importance of effective marketing in driving the success of your franchise. We are committed to supporting your marketing efforts by implementing a referral system that connects potential franchisees with the nearest location.

Our marketing team will work closely with you to develop targeted marketing strategies that will generate leads and attract potential franchisees in your area. Through comprehensive market analysis and segmentation, we will identify the most suitable target audience for your Mandarin learning program. By leveraging digital marketing, social media platforms, and local advertising channels, we will raise awareness of your franchise and drive interested individuals to reach out to you.

Through our referral system, we will actively refer interested parties to the franchise location closest to their area. This strategic approach ensures that you receive inquiries from potential franchisees who are geographically convenient for you to engage with. By connecting you with prospects who are in close proximity to your franchise, we aim to streamline the process and increase the likelihood of successful partnerships.

In addition to the referral system, we will provide you with marketing materials, branding guidelines, and ongoing support to help you effectively promote your franchise. Our marketing collateral, such as brochures, flyers, and digital assets, will showcase the benefits and features of your Mandarin learning program, highlighting its unique selling points and competitive advantages.

We believe in the power of localized marketing and the value of connecting franchisees with their target audience in their respective areas. By implementing a referral system and providing comprehensive marketing support, we aim to maximize your franchise's visibility, attract qualified leads, and facilitate the growth of your business.

Join our Franchising Program and let us collaborate in driving the marketing efforts for your franchise. Together, we will create impactful marketing strategies that will generate interest, increase brand awareness, and ultimately lead to the successful expansion of your Mandarin learning program.

Tai Chi Fitness Franchising Program

Welcome to Tai Chi Fitness, where we bring the ancient practice of Tai Chi to the modern world through our unique franchising program and comprehensive training.

Tai Chi Fitness is a recognized brand in the health and wellness industry, offering a range of programs and services that promote physical and mental well-being through the art of Tai Chi. With our franchising program, we invite passionate individuals and fitness enthusiasts to join us in spreading the benefits of Tai Chi to communities worldwide.

Our franchising program provides a turnkey solution for individuals looking to start their own Tai Chi Fitness business. We provide you with the necessary tools, resources, and support to establish and grow your franchise. Whether you are a seasoned fitness professional or a newcomer to the industry, our program is designed to accommodate different skill levels and backgrounds.

As a franchisee, you will benefit from our extensive experience and expertise in Tai Chi instruction and business operations. Our training programs are designed to equip you with the knowledge and skills needed to deliver high-quality Tai Chi classes and programs to your clients. We provide comprehensive training on the principles and techniques of Tai Chi, teaching methodologies, class management, and customer engagement.

Beyond initial training, we offer ongoing support to our franchisees. Our team of experienced professionals is always available to provide guidance, answer questions, and offer advice to help you succeed. We believe in fostering a collaborative and supportive network of franchisees, where we can learn from one another and share best practices.

One of the key advantages of joining our franchising program is the recognition and credibility that comes with being part of an established brand. Tai Chi Fitness has built a strong reputation for delivering exceptional Tai Chi experiences and achieving positive results for our clients. By becoming a franchisee, you leverage the trust and recognition associated with our brand, giving you a competitive edge in the market.

We are committed to the success of our franchisees and work diligently to create a mutually beneficial partnership. Our franchise program offers a flexible business model, allowing you to choose the scale and scope of your operations based on your goals and market demand. You have the freedom to customize your offerings and adapt to the unique needs of your local community.

Join our Tai Chi Fitness franchising program and embark on a rewarding journey of sharing the transformative power of Tai Chi with others. We invite you to explore this exciting opportunity and discover the possibilities of building a thriving business while promoting health and wellness.

Contact us today to learn more about our franchising program and start your journey towards becoming a part of the Tai Chi Fitness family.

Printed in Great Britain
by Amazon